DO YOU REALLY
BELIEVE?

"Are YOU A Believing Believer?"

Detrick L. Redding

Rome, GA ©2017

All scripture quotations are taken from the King James Version of the Bible.

Ephesians 2:8

For by grace are ye saved through faith; and that not of yourselves: it is the gift of God:

Hebrews 11:6

*But without **faith** it is impossible to please him: for he that cometh to God must **believe** that he is, and that he is a rewarder of them that diligently seek him.*

Table of Contents

INTRODUCTION

Imagine being in a Bible class of about 50-60 people.
Most people are regular church goers attending both
Sunday morning service and Wednesday night Bible
class. Of those present, we have Sunday school
teachers, choir members, missionaries, deacons, and
lay members, all of whom love God, their church and
each other. The Pastor starts a very riveting lesson
with a question that to me seemed easy but most
attendees were stunned. The question posed was
this... "If Jesus came tonight, even right now, who
would make it to heaven?" The pastor proceeded to
say, "All those who think heaven would be your home
right now, sit on the right side." As the people
pondered this, the pastor then said, "Those who think
they would not make it to heaven, sit on the left." I
was sitting on the left but to hear such a request, I got
up and immediately started shuffling to the other
side! Even though I was only 15, I confidently knew I
was heaven bound! It seemed as if I could not get to
the other side fast enough! Even the thought of
heaven excited me, so right side of the church, "Here I
come! I'm here with the heaven bound crew!" I look
beside me and my mom was there. Beside her sat
three of the mothers of the church. I looked in front of
me and there sat my older sister. I looked around and
surprisingly, less than TEN of us were in the group!
Where was everybody? On the left side! On the left
side of the church sat most of the crowd. I saw Sunday

school teachers, church leaders, and even preachers among the group. That baffled me. The teenage church boy that I was loved God and had a relationship with Him. I knew my salvation was secure in Jesus. My question was and is, how can most believers say they believe yet their actions say they have no confidence in my relationship with Christ?

Ephesians 2:8 says that we are saved by the grace of God through FAITH. Salvation is based on faith, not works. If this group or any group thinks, "My works are not up to par, so I may not make it." Then they have misinterpreted or completely misunderstood the scripture and its meaning.

In this easy to read book, we will delve into this concept of believing, having faith in God. It will change your life forever and for the better.

Chapter 1

The Simplicity
of
Faith

Faith in God is a simple, yet crucial concept. Hebrews 11:6 says that without faith, it is impossible to please Him. It is then safe to say, WITH faith we please God. As believers, we are to live by faith or in complete reliance on Him. Well, you may ask, you started this book with the term believe and with the title I ask "Do YOU Really Believe?" At first I use the term believe and now I am talking about faith. Faith in God is the same as believing in God. Having faith in God has become a superficial term that has been commercialized in the church world. At the same time believing God is minimized and made to look insignificant. Faith in God means believing in **God**. Here is a definition of faith I want us to hold onto:

Faith is an inward security in someone or something with or without tangible evidence.

To believe in God, we utilize the faith that God has measured out to us as stated in Romans 12:3. God responds to the need of many throughout the earth because of the people's faith in Him. We must come to God believing that He is AND that He is a rewarder of them that seek Him according to Hebrews 11:6. 2 Corinthians 5:7 tells us that as believers, we walk by faith or by our belief system and not by our natural reasoning or vision. Our inward security in Him, with or without tangible evidence, gets His attention. "God only responds to faith!" God does not respond to kicking, screaming, and crying. He responds to faith. God rewards diligent seekers of Him. What we believe in is important and **Who** we believe in is even more important.

Developing A Belief System

An inward security is desired by all. We look for it in so many different areas. We look for security in relationships. Jobs and job titles are used to pacify the desire. Pressure is unfairly placed on loved ones. This is all because of the need and desire for security. All of us have an inward cry for security, but when that source that we once thought was secure fails us, we are destroyed, hurt and angry.

Start examining yourself and others as well. Look at the woman in the relationship with an abusive man. She will not leave and not just because she is afraid of him. She is also afraid of being alone. It is the need for security. We look and see the man going to that factory job day after day. He is not fulfilled with the job but he has been there year after year. He has been pacified with that factory's check for years which has imitated security in his life. We all want something or someone to trust, and that thing or person that we trust provides us with a level of security that we long for.

"...God has dealt to every man a measure of faith" Romans 12:3. The ability to believe in or trust in someone has been given by God to the born-again believer. Now we must choose to trust God. In other words, we must develop a belief system. Romans 10:17

tells us more "faith comes by hearing and hearing by the word of God." We must be open to hear the Word of faith to increase in faith. We need to hear about the faithfulness of God to have faith increase in that area. We need to hear about the healing power of God to have faith increase in that area. The more we hear about God in an area, the more our faith increases about God in that area. The principle of "hearing to increase faith" is true for the negative as well. Whatever we hear in abundance will generate an inward belief system. If we hear long enough that failure is our only option; we are nothing; and we are insignificant; we will start believing it. We must be mindful of what we are allowing to enter through our ear gates. James 1:19 tells us to be *swift to hear* and *slow to speak*. When we listen to God and His words, we are developing a belief system in God and His word. This belief system will provide the security that is desired in us all.

Do You Believe?

Now from here on out, we are going to look at faith in detail. Remember the definition of faith given earlier

<u>*Faith is an inward security in someone or something with or without tangible evidence*</u>

Hebrews 10:38 says that we, as believers should live by our faith in God, not by reasoning; not by the

standards of the world, people or society, but by our faith in God. We live by faith and according to 2 Corinthians 5:7, we walk or proceed forward by faith. Walking in and living by our believing in God is vitally important. Romans 14:23 says that whatever is done outside of our faith in God is sin. You may ask, "What do you mean?" Once we do things that do not coincide with our belief system in God, that thing or things that we are doing become sin.

Faith To Believe For Salvation

Ephesians 2:8 says that we are saved by grace because of our faith. Romans 10:9-13 tells us the role of believing in salvation. It is believing in the death and resurrection of Jesus Christ. Believing leads us into a righteous position. Believing causes us not to be ashamed. The believing is an intricate step in salvation. No believing, no salvation. With believing, salvation is available. Salvation is not based on how good we are, how much we have changed, nor how much we do. It is based solely on our believing, combined with the salvation gift-giving of God. Salvation starts our believing lifestyle. Notice in scripture we are called Believers. To become a Believer, we must believe. Believing in the God of salvation starts the new life of a believer.

In my young 40 years of living, I have seen many that have claimed to meet the criteria. However,

I am still asking "do YOU believe?" Why do I ask that? My mind goes back to the Bible study at church that I talked about in the introduction. How can you say you believe and the evidence is not seen by outsiders nor is it seen by you yourself? St. Matthew 7:15-20 tells us that fruit, or the attributes of a person, reveal or convey who and what they believe. A good tree produces good fruit, a corrupt tree produces corrupt fruit. So, a believing tree produces believer's fruit!

The Importance of Fruit

We have discussed in the last section that fruit should follow a believer. I briefly want to explain why this is so important.

Romans 8:19 says that the earnest expectations of the creation waits for the manifestations (or the evidence) of the sons of God. There is an expectation in the earth for us as believers to display who we are. When we display who we are as believers, we give the onlookers hope and opportunity to rise up from where they are. Remember Jesus as He walked and displayed His belief in the Father. Lives were affected daily even until now.

James 2:14 gives us the second reason why a believer's fruit is so important. Listen, when the faith of a believer is not displayed, the believer's faith is dead faith. To be dead means to be unproductive. We affect nothing and no one with unproductive faith. Unproductive faith is a slap in the face of Jesus and a slap in your own face. That is why just being "church-goers" does not produce anything but religiously tired people with no joy, no peace, no happiness, and no assurance of heaven. So again, the two reasons why a believer's fruit is important:

1. The fruit that we display is intended to answer the cry of the whole creation.
2. The fruit that we display should produce results that change the earth!

Mark 16:15-18 is Mark's recording of the "Great Commission". The revelation that will come forth through these pages has an anointing to change your life. As you read these next five chapters, I recommend that you read slowly, following the scriptures that are given. Take time to meditate on the scriptures, writing down insight that God gives you. We are going to discuss five things that will change your life forever:

1.The Devotion of Faith

2. The Language of Faith

3.The Authority of Faith

4. The Walk of Faith

5. The Heart of Faith

MY NOTES:

Chapter 2

The Devotion

Of

Faith

Jesus gave the "Great Commission" to His disciples. He had walked with them for three and one half years. They witnessed numerous miracles, signs and wonders performed by the hands of Jesus. They had forsaken all to follow Him. Now as Jesus is climaxing His life and ministry on earth, He gives instructions for them to start their ministry.

Mark 16:15-16

"Go ye into all the world and preach the Gospel to every creature. He that believeth and is baptized shall be saved; but he that believeth not shall be damned."

They had the responsibility to preach to the world, encouraging them all to become believers. When one starts to believe, the salvation walk with Christ begins. It is the desire of God for all to come to repentance. Although this will not happen, He gives direct instructions to preach, giving all men the opportunity to hear so they can choose to believe or not to believe. Now, only God knows whether true believing has taken place in the heart. However, Jesus tells the disciples what to teach, and also what to look for in one that really chooses to believe.

Believer's Evidence

Verses 17-18 of Mark 16 will be our focus for a while. . . "And these signs or evidences will accompany them that believe; In my name shall they cast out devils; they shall speak with new tongues. They shall take up serpents; and if they drink any deadly thing, it shall not hurt them; they shall lay hands on the sick and they shall recover."

Romans 10:9 says "if we confess with our mouth the Lord Jesus and believe in thine heart thou shall be saved." The one thing about this scripture that has been overlooked is that part about confessing the **LORD** Jesus. The statement alone will change your life when embraced. Jesus must be confessed as Lord in and of our lives.

Lord- master, teacher, ruler; one in authority over

As we confess Jesus as Lord, we are naming Him Master, Teacher, and Ruler of our lives. I heard one of my father's in the Gospel say, Jesus is either Lord of all or not Lord at all. We must understand that there is no middle ground when it comes to Christ's Lordship in/of our lives. As Believers, we are adopted into the family of God (Galatians 4:5-6). It is our responsibility to become submissive children to our Father God. We declare His ruler-ship over our lives. As we do this, let us look at the first "believer's evidence".

1. *"In my name they shall cast out (all) devils"*

What are devils? Devils are outside forces/spirit beings that attempt to portray leadership in our lives through manipulation, guilt, and negative pressure. Since we have a Lord, when we declare His Lordship in Jesus' name, we eliminate or cast out all other gods or lords. As Believers, we must take inventory of our lives and see if there are any devils posing as God. Then we must cast them out in Jesus name! These gods can be people, loved ones, society's opinion, media's format, habits, drugs, ect. So believers must identify them and cast them out in Jesus' name! The devils will try to lay heavy on us trying to reel us in to their leadership. However, Hebrews 12:1 tells us to "lay aside every weight and sin which doth so easily beset us." As Believers, we declare "NO MORE in Jesus' name. Jesus is Lord! James 4:7 reminds us to "submit yourselves therefore to God. Resist the devil, and he *will* flee from you." Again, Jesus is Lord! Believers must be so devoted to God that no one or no thing lords over us.

Now take the next twenty-four hours to take inventory of you. Watch what you do automatically without thinking? What is it that controls your mood and your attitude? What habits have you not given up that plague you daily? That thing or that person need not control you any longer. God wants all of you. He is a jealous God...not jealous of you but jealous over you. God does not want to share His leadership position because He knows His way is right and He has your best interest at heart. Look at each issue that has tried to manipulate you and say boldly out of your own mouth the faith confession on the next page.

JESUS IS LORD OF MY LIFE. NO LONGER IS

(name whatever is attempting to lord over you)
LORD OVER ME. I CAST OUT ALL DARKNESS
FROM MY LIFE IN JESUS NAME!

Do this over every area of your life. As you pray, lift your hands in surrender to God and watch Him do things in your life by giving you power to change you. Declare this right now:

> *I am a believer and believers cast out all devils in Jesus name. All devils are evicted from my life, right now in Jesus name. Jesus is Lord!*

Giving God complete Lordship of your life is the first evidence of a believer. Notice I said *giving* God complete Lordship, because it is a daily process.

MY NOTES:

Chapter 3

The Language
Of
Faith

Did you know that faith people have their own language? We are calling it the language of faith. Jesus told the disciples in Mark 16:17 that the second thing or the second evidence that is associated with the believer is that the believer will speak with new tongues. I always assumed that this was speaking about the gift of tongues only. According to 1 Corinthians 12:8-11, the gifts are given by the Holy Spirit and divided out to every man as He wills. I'm like Paul in 1 Corinthians 14:18, I thank God, I speak with unknown tongues. Believers speak with new tongues AND with a new tongue. There must be a language change. Paul tells us in Ephesians 4:29 to "let no corrupt communication proceed out of your mouth." We must guard our mouths. We are now commissioned as Believers to speak gracious words and words that build up and not tear down.

As we grow as Believers, we must recognize that our hearts must be disciplined because our heart leaks through our mouths. The mouth can only reveal what the heart has in it. As Believers, we deliberately receive and apply God's word and God's grace to ourselves in order to speak God's word and speak grace to others. Our words will bring justice or condemnation to our lives. On purpose, we must guard the heart. Paul said it this way. What I believe, I speak (2Corinthians 4:13). We may say that we are Believers but our language or conversation and spoken words may say something else. We must take inventory of our mouths, our words and our heart. What are we saying without even thinking?

Recognize that we were created in the image of God the Father, Genesis 1:26. Everything that God wanted, He used words to create. The words of God carried creative power in them. We were created in that same likeness. That is why Solomon, the wisest man in the world past, present, and future said that the very "power of life and death" is in the mouth (Proverbs 18:21). What are you creating with your mouth? Listen, wisdom or foolishness is determined by what people say (Proverbs 15:1-2). Foolish words stir up anger and contention. Believers know that what they say represents who they are. Proverbs 15:4 becomes their foundation because they desire for their life to be a tree of life and they know that is what a wholesome word tree produces.

Believers line up their words with purpose. They recognize that what they say determines where they go. Words plant seeds into our lives that grow with time. Seeds do not necessarily grow overnight but they carry a long-term effect. That is why David said in Psalm 141:3 "Set a watch O Lord, before my mouth; keep the door of my lips." He was/is saying the significance of what I say is so important, Lord help me and my mouth!

Did you know that your words can stop God's plan from unfolding? In the book of Luke chapter one, Zechariah, the father of John the Baptist had to learn this principle. The Angel of the Lord came to him to inform him of what God wanted to do through him and his wife Elizabeth. God wanted to use them to bring forth John the Baptist to be the forerunner of Jesus. Elizabeth had been barren all her life and because of her age Zechariah was greatly surprised. He was very doubtful of the plan of God because of he and Elizabeth's inability to bear a child due to their old age. Now the Angel of the Lord told him that because of his reservation and his willingness to speak of the doubt-filled reservations, he would be dumb, unable to talk until the plan of God unfolded. I asked God why did Zechariah have to go through this and God let me know that He could not let him put words of doubt in the atmosphere. The plan that God had put in place, had to be performed. If Zechariah had not been stopped, the plan of God would have been hindered. We too can hinder God's plan by words of doubt. Zechariah was not able to talk until the baby was born and upon his agreement with God. In that day and time, it was custom to name the baby after the family, however, Elizabeth said his name shall be John. The ones present began to question such a request because no one in the family had that name. The people began to look to "the unable to talk" Zechariah. Zechariah motioned for a tablet and wrote, "His name is John." It was at that point that Zechariah's mouth opened and God loosed his tongue and he praised God. Zechariah was filled with the Holy Ghost that day and he prophesied with the hand of the Lord upon him. Would it not be easier for us if

God would do this to us? However, God wants us to choose His way of living and His way of speaking.

God's plan can and will come to pass in our lives IF we will agree with Him with our mouths. The key to this is finding out the plan of God through reading the Holy Scriptures, prayer, communication with God and by listening to the servants of God as they minister the Holy Word. Learn and know God's word and adjust your conversation to match what He is saying. Doubt and unbelief in our words negates the very plan of God. When we agree with God's word, we release His hands to do what He wants to do. Our language of faith becomes a language of reality. The believing of God's Word is released through our mouths.

David prayed it best in Psalm 19:14:

"Let the words of my mouth, and the meditation of my heart, be acceptable in thy sight, O Lord, my strength, and my redeemer."

David covered both areas in his prayer. Firstly, the words of his mouth…the words that come out of the mouth create life or death. We are satisfied or we experience what we say as seen in Matthew 15:11. Secondly, David covered the meditation of the heart. Whatever we meditate on long enough will come out of our mouths. Here the Psalmist cries out for help dealing with the heart because out of the heart flows the issues of our lives and its realities. As Believers, we do not live unto realities of the world but we live unto the reality of God's word.

Believers are ones who take their conversation seriously. When we speak against God's plan we inwardly get a check in our spirits conveying and warning us what is not appropriate. We need to immediately confess to God, ask for forgiveness according to 1 John 1:9. God will cleanse us from all unrighteousness or what is not right in His sight as we get into His word and meditate on what He speaks. We then embrace what He has said and we begin saying what He is saying. In other words, "we speak with new tongues" and speak the WORD ONLY.

Take some time right now and recall what you have been saying. Have I been speaking life or death, blessings or curses? Am I guilty of putting the wrong creative words out there for my family, my children and myself? Yes, I said your family and children. If you are a Believer, you have been given authority to speak into the lives of your family and children. You have a responsibility to them to speak life words over their lives. Those words must agree with you either way, positive or negative. If you speak life into your children's lives long enough and with authority and consistency, they will agree eventually! Their lives will begin looking like the life you have been speaking. Take ownership of your life by what you are saying.

Steps Toward the New Language

1. Admit the error of your language.

2. Commit some time to prayer (pray David's prayer in Psalm 19:14) and reading of the word. (I recommend going to your nearest book store and purchasing a Promise Book.)

3. Take your Bible (and Promise Book) and develop statements attaching you and the promises together and speak them out loud.

    Example: 1 Peter 2:24

    "Who his own self bare our sins in his own body on the tree, that we, being dead to sins, should live unto righteousness: by whose stripes ye were healed."

    With this promise, I could say, "No matter the symptoms of sickness, I am healed by the stripes of Jesus." That is not lying. That is simply agreeing with God. Another statement of faith that could be said is this, "I know I'm not perfect in myself, but I live in right standing with God and all sins are unproductive in my life in Jesus' name!" That's agreeing with His word.

4. Deliberately talk the new language daily and do it with boldness. Hebrews 10:19-23 tells us that we have complete access to God by

the blood of Jesus. We can boldly come to God and with full assurance in Him. We should hold firmly the confession of our faith without changing for anybody or anything.

Embrace the new language! Believers talk this way!

MY NOTES:

Chapter 4

The Authority

of

Faith

Let's look at Mark 16:17-18 again. "And these signs shall follow them that believe...they shall take up (remove) serpents..." The scripture here says that as believers we have the ability to take up serpents. Serpents throughout the Bible have always represented the evil one, the devil. The first evidence that we discussed was about denouncing the enemy as lord by declaring Jesus Christ as Lord. Now Jesus says that we take them up.

The enemy is constantly looking for someone to devour, someone to manipulate, someone to control (1Peter 5:8-9). The enemy appears to pose as a threat to the believer to cause fear anguish and frustration. The enemy desires to paralyze the believer. Guess what? Many believers have been paralyzed and I will tell you why. Most know that as Believers, we have power over the enemy in theory, but many never exercise that authority over him. That is what Jesus was talking about when He said that believers will "take up serpents." As Believers in God, we must activate the power of God in our lives in authority over the enemy and his influence.

Ephesians 6:12 tells us that WE wrestle against spiritual wickedness, principalities, and the rulers of darkness. We are to be combative against the enemy. Many have been passive Believers saying "Jesus will fix it after while." He cannot! Stop the madness! Jesus has done His work. It is now up to us! We put on the armor of God and become authoritative against the enemy. We do not go screaming, crying and hollering, but notice there is only one offensive piece of armor that we have and that is the sword of the Spirit. The sword of the Spirit is the Word of God. Therefore, Believers use the Word of God as a combative force against the enemy. Well, you may ask, is the Word of God able to do this? Yes, it is. Hebrews 4:12 says the Word of God is quick enough. The Word of God is powerful enough. The Word of God is sharp enough to do whatever is needed. Whatever it takes to destroy the enemy, the Word can do it. The key is that the Word must be applied against the enemy.

Are You Bound By the Enemy?

Matthew 12:29 gives us a picture of what is happening in the lives of some. No one can come into my natural house and steal my things with me being there unless they overpower me and bind me up or tie me up. I will not allow that! Well, spiritually we do not have to allow the enemy to come in and steal our inheritance. However, many have been bound by the enemy on their own territory. When the enemy binds a believer, he has every opportunity to take his stuff. The enemy's playground is our mind. Remember we wrestle against a spiritual enemy. The only area he can affect is your mind. If the enemy can get your mind, he can eventually get you!

Believers have been bound in their minds for years. Minds have been manipulated and brainwashed by the enemy. According to Romans 12:2, we must renew our minds to experience the good, acceptable and perfect will of God. This renewing of the mind will cause us to know God's real plan for our lives. When we know God's plan, we are empowered by God to protect our possessions, our children, and our lives from the evil one. God empowers us to resist the evil one. James 4:7 tells us to "submit...to God, resist the devil and he will flee."

1. Submitting to God is relinquishing ourselves to God and His Word. We must listen to the Lord for direction. Submission requires a dying to self and no longer controlling our own lives. The real you is your spirit and you should renew your mind to the point that your spirit gains ascendency over your mind, will and emotions. We must consciously lay ourselves down at the altar of the King by surrendering to His order and His **Word**. Yes, the Bible does say that we need to submit to one another and the scripture does say wives must submit to their own husbands. First, we are to submit to God. Not to a preacher first, but to God first. To submit to a person before we submit to God or without submitting to God is idolatry. Our God is a jealous God. He is the only One we should worship. Submission is the highest form of worship. Submitting to God

releases you of the responsibility of directing your life. The responsibility of directing something can be great and tedious. However, with submission, we rely on the leadership of God.

2. Resisting the enemy- we must resist the enemy. If we never resist the enemy, he will never leave! The enemy will leave when we properly resist him. We must resist the enemy steadfastly in the faith (1 Peter 5:9). How do we resist the enemy? We resist the enemy with the Word of God. Matthew 4 records the account of Jesus in the wilderness. After His forty days and nights of fasting, He was weak in the flesh. The enemy saw this as a perfect opportunity to tempt Jesus. The enemy came at Jesus three times trying to manipulate Him. The temptations dealt with lust of the eye, the pride of life, and the lust of the flesh. In all three, Jesus combated the enemy by declaring the Word of God. Notice, I said declaring the Word of God and not pouting the Word of God. So many times we quote a scripture, but we have no belief system in what we are saying. We must know and believe the Word that we are declaring. When we know the God of the Word, His Word becomes our Word. When the Word becomes our Word, we pronounce it with

boldness. "I AM HEALED!" "I HAVE VICTORY BECAUSE OF MY FAITH!" "I CAN DO ALL THINGS BECAUSE OF CHRIST JESUS STRENGTHENING ME!" Hallelujah!

3. Fleeing the Enemy- The enemy flees when he encounters a "believing Believer." (I like that term, believing Believer...will talk about it more a little later.) The believing Believer submits to God, resists the enemy properly and the enemy has no choice but to flee. The enemy cannot successfully defeat a Believer. The phrase, "flees from you," has been translated in some versions of the Bible to say, "run away as in terror". 1 Peter 5:8 says the enemy is "as a roaring lion." Notice it says, "as one", not "is one". He is a coward with a mask on trying to intimidate and imitate. When he sees that he can't intimidate, he flees. He will come back because that is what he does, but we must keep resisting him so he will keep fleeing as the defeated one that he is.

Authority Points

Deuteronomy 31:6-7

We are encouraged to be strong and of good courage. Also, here we are told to fear not. So often I have heard people make comments showing fear of the enemy. We are not to be fearful of the enemy. Remember he is "as a roaring lion". He tries to scare us, but we cannot be scared if we are of faith. Listen, God is with us.

1 John 4:4

God is with us and greater is He who is in us than any other force in this world. We must recognize that as Believers we have all of heaven backing us up. With God, we have the majority and "Majority Rules!" Glory to God!

Authority Lesson

To Do List:

1. Watch Out!

   We need to continually be on guard against the enemy. We cannot be ignorant of the devil's devices and tricks. He is a deceiver and we must guard against deception. The enemy is an accuser of the brethren and accusation brings condemnation. Condemnation is not of God. "Feelings" of condemnation should alarm us of the enemy's tactics. RESIST HIM. The more we know God and His Word, the more we equip ourselves against the evil one's tricks. The enemy knows God and His word, being that he is a fallen angel. He will twist the Word with the intentions of deceiving us. Jesus tells us to watch and pray lest we fall into temptation.

Revelation 12:10, Matthew 26:41

2. Stand Firm In Faith

We must be assured that the God we serve is backing us up. He is working with us. Is that not awesome to know? God is working alongside of us when we are combating the evil one. So, we must remain steadfast, immovable and always abounding in the works of the Lord knowing that our labor is not in vain. We must stay firm because wavering disqualifies us from receiving from God. This includes using authority over the enemy.

1 Corinthians 15:58, James:6-8, Matthew 12:25

3. Maintain Your Ground

The scripture says, "quit you like men" in 1 Corinthians 16:13, which translates into maintaining your ground. We must take charge of ourselves, our possessions, our children, our families, our churches, and our communities. We have a spiritual responsibility to others around us. The enemy has no right to things that do not belong to him. Why is he taking over our children? It is because no one has taken spiritual authority over the enemy. We have been taking deadly blows from the evil one. The time is now. We must not be passive anymore. Take charge over your life, your family, your children, your community and your church. Strike the enemy. Do not wait until his attack. Place a hedge of protection around your stuff with the Word of God.

Genesis 4:9, Romans 8:19, Ephesians 4:27

4. Be Strong

Be strong in the Lord and in the power of His might. We cannot be foolish and combat the enemy in ourselves. We cannot stop the enemy with our strength, but with God's strength, we can. Do everything in the name of JESUS! At the name of Jesus every knee must bow. The devil trembles at the mention of the name. As you resist the enemy, know that the enemy needs to hear the name JESUS! Remember the name of the Lord is a strong tower.

As we conclude this chapter, know that the enemy needs to hear you resist him. He will never flee if you never resist. The enemy has no right to eat your lunch, so do not let him. God gave to you areas of responsibility of which you are to maintain proper stewardship. If the enemy takes it and brings any lasting harm to any of it, you have not been a good steward. Today is the day to take charge and take up serpents in Jesus name!

MY NOTES

Chapter 5

The Walk

of

Faith

Mark 16:17-18

"These signs shall follow them that believe...if they drink any deadly thing, it shall not hurt them..."

Here Jesus informs the disciples that Believers have a wonderful testimony of protection from deadly things. Great promise! I am just imagining this deadly thing to be something like poison. However, for the word deadly to be used signifies the purpose of this thing. The creating of something like this has the intent to kill and destroy. The deadly thing that Jesus talks about, a Believer can drink it and will be fine. Its intentions were to bring death to the Believer. In reading this, leaving it in the natural realm gives me reason enough to praise God. Hearing that God will naturally protect me when I drink poison, brings a smile to my face. I believe God can do this but what about many years ago when people drank a poisonous substance because a person instructed or forced them to drink? The purpose of drinking it was to kill and it worked. This leads me to believe there must be a spiritual connotation to this part of the scripture. Look at the phrase "any deadly thing." Spiritually to be dead means to be separated from God without any hope. Here Jesus is saying if a Believer gets hold of something that is intended to separate them from God, it will not work! Hallelujah! Glory to God! Notice Jesus said "if". "If" signifies that the subject is not a normal or common occurrence. Whatever the subject is, it is not something done on a regular basis.

Christ Jesus our Lord and Savior died for our sins. Before His death, Christ lived on earth as an example of righteousness for us to follow. We are to live unto righteousness (I Peter 2:21-25). Jesus tells us in Matthew 6:33 to "seek first the Kingdom of God and His righteousness." We have the responsibility and privilege to find out the way of God for our lives. What is *His righteousness?* It is HIS way of doing and being right. We are to seek the way of God to live the way of God. We should be swift to hear, slow to speak, slow to wrath (James 1:19-21). Swift to hear means to be ready to hear God at any time. Slow to speak means do not let your mouth go untamed, keep a watch over your mouth. Being slow to wrath means we should be mindful not to allow our emotions to get the best of us, not let our emotions rule us. Our spirits need to be in ascendency. Why is this so important? The wrath or emotions of man does not know or do the righteousness of God on its own. We must receive and apply the Word of God to our lives to live out the Word. We have to want to live in righteousness in order to do it. As believers, we need to be doers of the Word and be led by our spirits, not our emotions. Do the Word that you know to do. Get more Word, and then do it. I am not saying we will ever get it down perfectly; however, daily we are to put forth a good faith effort to do the Word and walk righteously before the Lord. Now to do this, is really for our benefit because the Word empowers us to prosper.

Obedience to the Word of God is right. However, disobedience is sin. To be disobedient to the order of God is sin (1 John 2:1-5). Now, look at Romans 6:23. The penalty of sin is death. Remember what death is ...spiritually separated from God. Sin places a barrier between us and God. Oh yes, the "deadly thing" from Mark 16 has the same intentions of separating us from God! I submit to you that the "deadly thing" that Jesus talks about is sin. I know that is challenging some of your sanctified mindsets right now. Keep your heart open.

God has called us to walk in the integrity of the Word. We should be doers of the Word and not hearers only. As we walk in the integrity of the Word, we maintain our righteous position. We must habitually walk in compliance with our God, the King. Romans 2:7-11 tells us that glory, honour, and peace comes to EVERY believer that does good and does what is in the Word.

The Deadly Thing

Mark 16:18 "...and if they drink any deadly thing, it shall not hurt them..." The key word here is "*if*". If conveys that it is not a habitual behavior or ongoing. A Believer walks in the integrity of God. Demons tremble when a Believer gets up in the morning knowing and walking in that integrity. Angels stand at our beckoning call when we speak and act in that integrity... God watches over us, so if by chance the enemy convinces a sin upon a child of God, God says, "my grace is sufficient." Glory to God! To be perfect is a tall order, but to strive for perfection knowing that the enemy cannot take me out at one wrong move, that is glorious! It will not be "when" we mess up. It is only "if" we mess up, because we strive for righteousness all the way! However, when we know the glory, honour, and peace that is on us, we negate the plan of the enemy and that is comforting.

-*The glory that is upon us defeats the penalty of sin.*

-*The honor that is upon us, removes the guilt of sin.*

-*The peace that is upon us, negates the separation of sin.*

MY NOTES

Chapter 6

The Heart

of

Faith

Mark 16:17-18

"And these signs shall follow them that believe… they shall lay hands on the sick, and they shall recover."

The last evidence of this teaching deals with the motives or the intentions of the heart. Here Jesus reveals the heart of a Believer. The Believer has a heart for others. Jesus says that they lay hands on the sick. Genesis 48:14 reveals that the laying on of hands was done to transfer blessings and to anoint. To lay hands on another requires a selfless and giving attitude (James 2:14-18). We as Believers should look for opportunity to lay hands.

Jesus said that believers lay hands on the sick. The sick are the ones that are infected by an internal or external germ, a foreign trespasser that causes the body to operate outside its normal God ordained character and functionality. Physically and spiritually, sick people have symptoms that vary due to the type of sickness. With a cold-trespasser, people deal with congestion, sneezing and coughs. When dealing with the foreign invader called flu, people encounter fever, aches, and cold chills. The intensity of the sickness causes varied symptoms. Physical and spiritual sickness follow the same suit…to invade, steal and destroy. Sometimes it is hard to realize, but when we encounter spiritually sick people, they too have symptoms not always detected. These symptoms vary from bad attitudes, disrespectful behaviors, walls of hatred and meanness, the need to defend self, the need to prove one's self, etc. and all because of a spiritual sickness. We were all created with the need for God and for security. And when God is not in the equation of our lives, we act out in different ways. I am sure that we all have come in touch or proximity to at least one spiritually sick person every day. We have sick people on our jobs, in our families and in our schools. Some are sick of sin, sick of hurting, sick of pain, sick of rejection, sick of loneliness, and just sick of being sick. Physical sickness and spiritual sickness are both real and both must be addressed.

Who are Sick Among You?

James 5:13-14

Pastor James tells us when we have sick among us, we need to be the church and pray for them anointing them with oil. The sick need us, the Believers in God, to lay hands on them. Remember laying on of hands was a transferring of blessing and releasing favor upon another. We must be willing to and we must transfer blessings upon others. Again, this requires selflessness. We must refuse to operate in selfishness.

Let's talk about the symptoms some more. The symptoms of the sickness will cause the body to do different things which in turn causes the emotions of the affected to react adversely. We must keep this in mind as we approach sickness and people presenting symptoms of sickness. Not all the effects of sickness are tolerable. Some reactions will be a challenge to us. We must gird ourselves with the knowledge of our purpose so that we will not become frustrated. Believers will still lay hands on the sick.

What Does Laying On Of Hands Look Like?

Matthew 5:38-48

In these verses of scripture, Jesus teaches on retaliation and love. As Believers, we must resist the opportunity to retaliate. We must give and not always try to take. Verse 44 is a key scripture for us. Four things are commanded of us...

Love, Bless, Do Good To, and Pray For

We should love our enemies!

We should bless them that curse us!

We should do good to them that hate us!

We should pray for them that despitefully use us and persecutes us!

Why should I do all of this? Well, because they are sick people and they probably do not even know it. This is very different in comparison to the society we live in today, and to people in general. To leave retaliation to God can be difficult, however vengeance is mine says the Lord! What about my pride, my reputation, and my ego? We must leave all of that at the door. These things cannot be the focus of a Believer. We must believe God enough to do things His way and do it with full assurance that HE has our backs. That leads me to Ephesians 5:21. Paul tells the believer to submit ourselves to each other in reverence to God. We have no need to fight with one another when we believe God. We trust Him wholly enough to obey and to release control.

Romans 12:9-21

Paul shares a lot here in this teaching about Christian brotherhood. We are to let our love be real. He instructs us to be kind and affectionate to one another. Not only kind, but we are to show kindly affection. Love and kindness can be spoken, but to display it through affections is selfless for the giver and fulfilling for the receiver. Even in business, we as Believers must not be lazy and continue in prayer for the brethren. We are to distribute to the saints who are in need and show hospitality to others. When others curse us, we are instructed to bless them. We are to provide things that are honest in the sight of men and live peaceably with ALL men. We are not to avenge ourselves or seek revenge. What about our enemies? We are instructed to feed them when they are hungry and give them something to drink when they thirst. Do not be overcome by, or with, the evil of others but DO overcome their evil with our good, Paul says. I am not going into much detail because the one of the concepts of doing good to others, loving them, and honoring them is laying your hands on them. You are blessing them. Romans 12:20 says that we heap coals of fire upon their heads when we do good to our enemies. And that is a good thing! The goodness that we do is searing their very consciences-bringing about healing to their wounds. The wounds have been open scars because others have gotten too frustrated at the outward showing of sickness and never wanted to deal with the sickness itself. We have been assigned to some sick people. They are waiting on us to lay hands on them. Will you lay hands on them?

I dare not forget to mention physically sick people. Healing of the physical body is God's will. There is much in God's Word that plainly tells me so; therefore, I believe it. One of my biggest desires is for mentally ill people to be healed. I believe that I will see that in my lifetime. Also, for a child of God to walk around sick with high blood pressure, diabetes, cancer, asthma, and any other sickness does not bring glory to God. To be able to live, operate and minister through these sicknesses is commendable and I believe God is glorified when a person pushes through these things. However, to be completely healed of cancer, high blood pressure, diabetes or any sickness gives God the ultimate glory that is due His name. Believing Believers lay hands on the sick through prayer!

The second part of laying on of hands as evidence is that "they shall recover." Glory to God! As Believers, we lay hands on the sick, whether physically or spiritually, and they SHALL recover. How can I make such a claim? Mark 16:20 tells me that the Lord works WITH a Believer to confirm His Word. God's power hooks up with my application of prayer and kindness to manifest whatever healing is needed. There is no limit to this because there is no limit on our God. Ephesians 3:20 says "...according to the power that works in us", a believer can do "above all that we could ask or think." Further, "...the sufferings of this present time are not worthy to be compared with the glory that shall be revealed in us", the believing Believers (Romans 8:18). Not only in heaven, but the glory shall be revealed on earth when I, we, lay hands on the sick and they recover. Believers, we must refuse to stay in the natural realm, because things that are present are always subject to change (2 Corinthians 4:18). After reading this, I believe Holy Spirit will begin prompting you to lay hands (Philippians 2:13) on the sick and they shall recover. Follow the prompting. Believers believe enough to do whatever God says do. It is not my/our job to make the sick recover, but it is God's.

As I close this chapter, let me finish my point from Pastor James. In James 5:13-16, God lets us know that we will have sick folds among us. So, we are not to get frustrated with sick folks. Look at it this way, God allowed them to be around you because He knew that there is an anointing on your life to deal with the sickness and get them healed by the Healer. James tells us to call for the elders of the church to pray for the sick. Do you know who elders are? They are proven Believers. Since we are "believing Believers" and have gotten this far in the book, we are now proven. We are to be the church NOW and pray for the sick. Look at what our prayers do:

1. Save the sick

2. Raise up the sick

3. Bring forgiveness for sins

We pray for each other to be healed.

"The effectual fervent prayer of a righteousness man availeth much." James 5:16

As a believer, we are declared to be the righteousness of God in Christ Jesus. So, this verse is referring to us and our prayers. Our effectual fervent prayer is simply intentional, heartfelt prayer. Why is that simple? As Believers, we mean business when we pray, or at least we should. I listen and am slow to speak, so when I speak I have something to say and my prayer is communicating to God. Now James concludes here by saying "availeth much" which means much power is made available. When a believer prays for others that are sick, we are making much power available for them to step right into their healing.

Look at your own life right now. Are there some sick folk that you have overlooked? Did you turn your nose up on a sick man on the street? Have you given up on a sick family member? What about on your job? In your church? In your community? Go lay hands on them. God will cause them to recover.

MY NOTES:

Chapter 7

A Believing

Believer

To believe is a part of our make-up. Each of us believes in something. Romans 12:3 says that we have been given a measure of faith. God imparted faith into us. Let me prove it to you. If you are not sitting, go sit in your favorite chair. If you are already sitting, go prop up against a counter or something. We generally do not go through an inspection of the chair or the counter. Think about it...did you examine the legs, brackets, and screws on the chair questioning whether it would hold you before you sat in it? Did you push at the counter to see if it would give way before you put your entire weight on it? Did you take your car through a seven point inspection everyday last week before you would even crank it to leave for work? To be honest, none of us did these things. We just simply sat down in the chair, leaned on that counter, and jumped into the car expecting it to do what it is supposed to do. That is a level of faith!

Now our salvation started with this same principle but it is the God-kind of faith and His faith is supernatural. "By grace ye are saved through faith" (Ephesians 2:8). Salvation is obtained through faith in Jesus and is not based on works nor our own ability to do anything or make ourselves right. I do not change myself to be saved, but because I am saved I give attention to myself for change. My faith is crucial in the salvation plan. No faith, no salvation.

Since faith is at the beginning of our walk, we should hold on to and grow our faith throughout the duration of our lives on earth. 1 Peter 1:13 tells us to hope until the end. Hebrews 3:14 tells us to hold our confidence steadfast all the way to the end. We MUST remain in faith. This is a challenging area for me because so many start their Christian walk of faith with a genuine heart towards God becoming believers in Jesus Christ as Savior. They truly believe God raised Jesus from the tomb for their salvation, however, somewhere down the road, some stop believing. There are a lot of church-goers that attend church regularly, contribute their monies and time, but have stopped believing a long time ago. 2 Peter 2:21-22 compares this behavior to a dog returning to its own vomit. It appears to be easy to believe for salvation and it is easy. It is a heart issue. However, do not stop there but increase your faith to believe for all that God has to offer. Believe God for total deliverance. Believe God for complete restoration of family. Believe God for complete healing. We need to increase our faith, increase our believing. We have a measure of faith, however (more) faith comes by hearing and hearing of the Word of God (Romans 10:17).

Failing to increase in faith is a sin against God and self

To rely on and trust in God is pleasing to Him; to do the opposite is not pleasing to Him. Jesus told Thomas, "Blessed are we, when we believe even though we do not see." Blessed means empowered to prosper, so when a man believes, He is empowered and equipped with God's ability to prosper. We must become "believing Believers" refusing to stop believing. When we believe in God, we will receive from God everything that the relationship has for us.

Do You Really Believe?

In the book of Matthew, there is an occurrence of two blind men who confronted Jesus for healing. In the gospels, there are many instances of healing and miracles. However, this caught my attention and caused me to examine myself and to even write this book. In Matthew 9:27-31, two blind men followed Jesus and cried out for mercy. Jesus continued into the house of destination and the men continued to follow inquiring mercy of Him. Jesus turned to those me and asked, "Believe ye that I am able to do this?" This surprised me. It seemed to me that what they had done already by following and inquiring of Jesus made this question about believing a no brainer. They followed Jesus. They cried out to Him and showed persistence. This appeared like belief to me. However, He still asked, "Do you believe I can do this?" So many times, we can appear as believing Believers but deep down in the heart we have missed something. These two blind men appeared to pass the test. However, for Jesus to ask even after they appeared to believe through an outward showing, makes me think. This tells me that there is a chance of unbelief even when I appear to be crossing every "t" and dotting every "i".

We have a lot of church-goers that look like they are Believers, but do they really believe. This book is not intended to bring condemnation to the body of Christ but to convince the body of Christ to examine themselves, confess, and repent to please God. Do you really believe? Look at the evidences of believing again. Make efforts to add to your faith, virtue and to your virtue, knowledge; to knowledge, add temperance; and to temperance, add patience; to your patience, add godliness; and to godliness, add brotherly kindness and to brotherly kindness, add charity. For the Word says if all these things be in you and abound, they will not make you barren nor unfruitful (2 Peter 2:5-8). When we do this, we are making our calling in Jesus and His election of us sure or we get what we are proving through our believing.

I am taking steps to add to my faith so that I will have an answer when Jesus asks "Do you really believe?" Yes Lord. I do believe. If you were on trial right now for being a Believer, the prosecutor and defense would both have some things to submit to the court as evidence. You are now in a great position to defend your faith. Will there be enough evidence to prove your stance? Jesus is asking even now, "Do you really believe?"

Prayer of Salvation &

Baptism in the Holy Ghost

Friends, the Word of God tells us in *Acts 2:21 & 38*

"And it shall come to pass, that whosoever shall call on the name of the Lord shall be saved... Repent, and be baptized every one of you in the name of Jesus Christ for the remission of sins, and ye shall receive the gift of the Holy Ghost."

Pray this prayer by ***faith,*** and receive a new life NOW in Jesus Christ and be filled with His Holy Spirit with the evidence of speaking in tongues.

Father God, I come to You in Jesus name believing that what Your Word says is true. I call on the name of the Lord Jesus so that I can be saved NOW. Jesus, I pray and ask you to come live in my heart and be my Lord and Savior according to Romans 10:9-10. That "If thou shalt confess with thy mouth the Lord Jesus, and shalt believe in thine heart that God hath raised Him from the dead, thou shalt be saved. For with the heart man believeth unto righteousness; and with the mouth confession is made unto salvation." I confess and believe that Jesus Christ is Lord and Savior of my life and that God raised Him from the dead! I am now a born again Christian. I am Your child and I am saved. You said in Your word "If ye then, being evil, know how to give good gifts unto your children; How much more shall your heavenly Father give the

Holy Spirit to them that ask Him?" (Luke 11:13). I am asking you to fill me with the Holy Spirit. Rise up in me Holy Spirit! Hallelujah! I praise You God Almighty! I fully expect and thank you for the ability to speak with other tongues as Your Spirit gives me the utterance (Acts 2:4).

Now, you praise and thank God for filling you with His Holy Spirit. As you begin to hear words or syllables deep in your belly, that are not your natural language, SPEAK THEM OUT! Use your own voice. God will not force you to say anything. No matter how strange the sounds are, speak them! It is your God-given heavenly language and it is empowering (Jude 20)! Continue daily to pray in your heavenly language for you are now a Spirit filled believing Believer!

Pray and ask God to lead you by His Spirit to a church home where you can hear the preached Word of God. It is vital that you get connected with the Pastor and church family God has for you (Hebrews 10:25).

Toris and I would love to hear from you on your new life in Christ! Or if you have a testimony from reading this book that you would like to share! Contact us or find out about upcoming meetings and events via:

Website: **Rallyupministries.org**

Email: **Rallythechurch@rallyupministries.org**

Mail: **P.O. Box 1044, Rome, Ga 30162**

FB: **facebook.com/Rallyupministries**

We love you and are excited about the plan of God for you!

About the Author

Detrick Redding is a lifelong resident of Rome, Ga along with his wife Toris and four (4) children: Antarius, Jamal, Jara, and Charity. He and Toris are founders and pastors of Rally UP Ministries, Inc. Dedicated to providing others with excellent service, time and resources, he was also Assistant General Manager at the Chick-fil-A Dwarf House for over 20 years. Active in his city, he completed the Leadership Rome program through the Greater Rome Chamber of Commerce in May 2011; served as chairman of the South Rome Redevelopment Board for three and a half years, resigning to take the post for Rome City Commissioner; previously served on the Board of Boy Scouts of America; and served on the Board of Directors for the North West Georgia Housing Authority.

After serving two local churches for 12+ years in youth and teen ministry, God began giving Detrick a vision and mission to ***"Build Lives in Order to Build the Kingdom of God"*** through Outreach Ministry and teaching the Word of God. Then in 2010, the Spirit of God began directing him to Pastor the church to further build the body of Christ and win souls. Finally in 2016, the Lord called he and Toris back into the field ministry where they continue to travel preaching and teaching the uncompromised Word of God.

Detrick knows what it means to have to learn and grow in believing God. Having been reared in a home by a strong faith filled mother, a dedicated father and born again at the age of ten himself, Detrick learned to trust and BELIEVE God, as he administered the Word like medicine three times daily to himself at age 16 as instructed by his mother. At that time a debilitating virus attacked his spine causing him to not be able to walk or speak clearly. Hospitalized, doctors worked to find out the problem but came up with no answers, neither a cure. Sent home from the hospital with a bag of medicines and prescriptions, his mother told him he was of age and had to make a choice to take the medicine or stand on the word and BELIEVE God for himself. He chose to BELIEVE God.

Having ministered the Word of God with all boldness locally and abroad, Detrick is a preacher, teacher and lover of the Word of God. He has a uniquely anointed ability to preach and teach with simplicity and depth causing revelation into and desire to live out the character and ways of God. By the Christ in Him, Detrick builds the hearers of God's anointed word, imparting the same wisdom, knowledge and power of God to believe and receive healing, deliverance and the abundant life of God.